Daniel Farnan

Poems

Poems
by Daniel Farnan
©2025 Daniel Farnan

Publisher: Duncan Dobson

American Poetry Systems
South San Francisco
California

www.apsssf.com

APS#002
Revised Second Edition
10 8 6 4 2

Cover Art: Detail from *Long Spring*
by Daniel Farnan and Duncan Dobson.

ISBN 979-8-218-09762-2

Poems

by
Daniel Farnan

Tread Upon Trodden Trail

Odd to let go and
live to meet
A memory.
So long or gone in
thrice as many nows.
The comfort of it
reminding mystic pacing
of further places and
of nearer jogs.
Not just once from
long ago – the sin
and the song
of silence.
Silence left behind,
not unquestioned –
in silence by the other
half
of a human Pattern –
genuine; humane
echoing love.

Life can be so silly
Like Irish Devils cavorting
a new conspiracy of hope
as the music is still
and lovely maidens dance
Alone in imagination

The BlackInk, if not enough
will still record the lies
only to laugh as hard
and wake the day filled
inside and out; parade

Yes, Let us parade ourselves
so simply and for even
that the chemistry of the Sun
Will not bely its making
And in truth speak of 'hope'

Fickle Finger oh gruesome
Shifting playout, all too plain
how astoundingly nonplussed
to see the bleeding red
bleeding edge
of recent writ verse
edited by a hated spill

yet fickle still sense
from wash and dry
another to me whole recovered
in pages torn apart
by the spinning whine

Some edits come from fear
others can so conquered do
relating's lesson lost again

Let the racing horses run
watching them athrong
as the rider's course
and spectators Laugh
see the faith of life resound
and the filling of it making

Yet sallow Fields tilled
as oft in times of old
So simply the caring ceiling
turns the glass to gold
When the simple people gaffe
there is only God waiting

There without rod but staff
to stand serene of manner
quietly setting pace
reminding chaotic humans
of more than human race
and still a comfort slightly

Shadowed nearby patterned
a black eagle flies
and a hawk to prey soon
Pelican, seagulls

and the sun shining on China Beach
Tempted again to swim
with weeks to go before
another election

The welcoming future
and clear skies seem
as nearer

Stalks from the ground
streak up
as layered patterns
compose

Stand for deliverance
as I did and catch the bus
Fast-turning schedules
as that dinosaur
seldom slow

Loud musics of life
and some quiet joys
taken in passive regard
in view of surprise
and surprises

Some unsettled sublime
to seeming select
as a future running late
followed forward well
reminded me late
of sufferings owned

Which conspired to a smile
of a quieted noticed delight

Does Dirty Donny take a knee
like his hand a pussy grasp
or as if Ivana wanna
Lincoln. Bedroom. Snap.
No No not Hence, Donny's got
Mike Pence!
Onna first class flight
to really ugly plain insite
the very trauma'd tiny white
to buy the guns and glee
Sink in quicksand, quick
and wonder where's the love
But is it really gay day play
Divorcee? Or used entrée?
Like Hugh Hefner's tits
tickled Sports Illustrated bits
in recovered Swimwear lit
by those funky sounds
like Vladimir Putin all downtown
asking for a ride
from Pussy Riot
or finding the Beatles
underground, on Airforce 1;
Blue Angels playing fun
for a Million Dollars –
in travelled gas and
Kim Jong Un needs a hand
Too

grab it rabbit
Saigon Hotel
and a Salad Bar gone to Hell
with a carroty stink
as if you think
a Peachnik would apologize
when you call the lies
by clapping back
like Bill Gates was selling crack
to a broken Africa

Blues Clews News
Bear-an-steen Bear
nothing there

yet
from some cotel room bar
See Harvey Weinstein fat
and naked in a shower
the currency has the power
to by-ugly make you leave
So for America
Do not grieve
Pop another Alleve
And to the flying shoes receive
the fire from delight
in a quiet night
no nuclear identity
will power coloniality
in Puerto Rico's hour

of need
indeed
So small it is to laugh
At the fearless leader's gaffe
of Boris and Natasha
Rocket man, Rocket squirrel
Come on now just give the whirl
and go to college like a girl
for stem cells after midnight
and neither Merkel nor Macron
will plan to homey keep it on
as oil for arms marches long
for Bitcoin in the daylight.
now in your loved self-driving car
that you may well call bizarre
The emptying of water
and so we all may board the Flight
to a Future out-of-sight
and Facebook Post to friend of night
this dire and perverse-est plight
of a Government that only might
Oligarch's Plutocracy.
So to meaning you and me
erase the health and taxes
While online all the faxes
Without paper
Just slow my email down

Development of
Relationships in
Shared Values.

Be direct about the
meaning to Oneself.
Elude "Agent §"
in the Goal/Mission.

"Imagine a Disaster
with no help."

①Issues
②Impact
③Potential for Involvement

Fresh ideas
          Information
Respect existing
          Philanthropes

Encourage.
Succeed.
Encouraged.
Make Champions.

In this room again
the walls the same, else changes
over this strife, my life
some of me lingers here
in more of nadir's close
like kicking hope to start.
herein the shift improved
and as Thomas I feel the heart
through my wounds
it beats somehow
and the hill of not demeaned
has bright astroturf
and smiling garden gnomes
these Shepherds are less wrought
and even bear a smile
a gas station convenience
sits in prison's waiting rooms
speaking in tongues
I could bathe in the waters
cried over histories
dragged-in, here over decades
What more to speak of
when polite lines are even'd
and the walk up the slide
less steep
of my life, life has learned
and as slow these steps
still as boots in mud
now stone
my feet must be fitted

it is only this human
optimistically as art
to move to more of grace
that seen-in reasoning
weighted and lifted
as Honor's gravity ekes
and that sought peeks
like a Cheshire Cat's smile
winking

Reanimate
Discourse or Power
Replace the Now
Denial no disorder
Regenerate
Conclusions at the guns
Repatriate
The unmoving to the day

Disparate
Motions make the now
Like the overboard
clawing up lifeboats
without help in.

A swan shines
in water
under ripples reflecting sunrise
uttering at last the song
of one long note
'Stay, think of me.'

A Full Circle

Like one Hundred years ago
or maybe one Thousand,
I was here in a shifting
Morass.
A Shifting Morass of folk
Behind it, a spectre plain
not just **my** spectre.
Like an apportioned storm
set in motion alone
that drew dire attention.
Those keys jangle now.
Just for me.
A full circle
Sees a circle open
the broken trust, revealed
revilingly backward - wrong
reflecting the last, this, play
in a 'game,' no games!
Played by last century's other fool.

MDMA last night
At dinner my rage
at last
reflecting democracy
descending fast

The show of yesteryear's jog
reminding of self as a boy
Picasso & his contemporaries
Lit up the rooms

This morning at last
I know my exoneration
7 years a long time
to be rent for no crime

The longer time's weight
lifting at Last
as the long weights
seem to slip away.

Future's brightness again
at last
25 years to call the past
The intensity of it all is
still a fraught nationalism
My own efforts withal.
Encounter my present tense

Some sense of it
Some help of it
Get the sadness and deep
Call forth the less lightness
given the present tense

The right things done
The spirit awake
The long river of it
Truth in body paid
Clarity a dear thing aft

The Harangue of Sadness
was tagging me deep
to the edge of tears
this silent force
A sadness as much at
experience as our Loss
Yet a forward motion
Continuing climbs
and an effort still made
toward the goal as such
tiring me deeply too
has smoothed my way
Age will come still yet
but for now my strengths
still enough get me alive
and well. About death's grace
So it goes in a difficulty
The context of some's living
step beyond the bounds

So oddly light
in the weighted gardens
Gardens floral in the sun
gardens of human growth
askance the processes, those
of a generation's aside
"Yes, we are human too!"
Resounding like creativity
From even the least
At table, shows ability
And fades, and joins the
Parades both day & night!

The clarity of sunlight
Almost laughing
finds a day's beauty
an ease of care in air
Lacking the crashing of
Wildness too is serene
on this warm for basking
promising love for the asking

Reasons
to leave or stay home
The 5 is a long wait.
The 21 is worse one-way
The cost is more, often, than
Return.
The question of social stability
resolved in nomadic payoff –
each new society a learner,
It is prohibitive to enjoy
the reasons to stay
For all of the above stays.

The Power of Place

So many times I recall
My lone-styled journeys
into a hope of welcome
so sadly to know its need alone
So difficult most of many tries
The passages made full each
to remind only of returns
such a complexity is unfair
Yet, each time space was
each time the call to mind
to myself the joy anticipated
was kept whole, unenjoyed
just a gift well wrapped
offering a subsequent
comfort, discerning
The wrack as the time, seen through
Leaving in its wake ruin
provides ample opportunity
to see what should have been
and what band-aid is now
Just hard-sided of arcane.
The Clocktower Rang out
Clanging Bells Clappered out
The lover's momentous half
not just for me.
As once they were designed
The bells rang out the time
For all to hear.

Essentials Run

Ran, Ran Xerox
along to Clorox
lovely detox, bleach
cleaning the Pandemic

Click that second hand
and minute men too
clicking as hours meet
shading the Doppler daylight

a greeting gathered
with bodies slathered;
in close distanced stance
to see and be with others

What is important shows
even as laughter slows
into the sounds of dreaming

Which humane reason
recreates hope
in a form of forward motion

Wherein a true all
Can find the real ease
With and without arcata

Such a drama to sense
The forward motion slow
And reframe itself again

Wandering, not lost
Awash in tidal seas
The pearl below and above

Branches stem in one.
More of sense than loss
to find the hope of love.

Transparency is
invisibly a multiphone
asking for all Truths
by showing clarity
metaphorical charity
Intra-Sounding Regency
methodology
From transparency a filial
literacy incomplete, open
The formative excuse comes
as unasked for and quiet
Transparent not Innocent
Lingua Pura

Trans   Parent

Foiling the lies uneven
Passive Present

Longo   long ago welcomed
all wearied motorists across
a great crossing
Accomplishment
Anticipated ease abatement
Longo Long Ago Human Ideal
Bracing Strutting Arches Real
At last to Longo
Like Heaven's Gate Earthly
A power after powers
on a crescendo'd way
Longo Long   a   go
So briefly to pass challenge
Intensity of thought and
Message wrought through

Enumerated Truths
offer no more or less
success
without sense
The difficulties do not
disperse by themselves
often the great success
too large to discern
is radically avoided
as another bait-sized treat
is seized instead
Perhaps the mythological size
of the great goal
is so grand a presence
Its provenance ascribed
to myth alone rather
than to the accomplishment
Heroic, real, inherent
that goals achieved embody

Again…

Social Quixosis,
abrogating a quiet joy.
Friendliness, warmth.
The active of humankind
Plain, and kind
Again, wondering not only
at myself engaging
and finding pleasure
in human kindness
also, a disappointment
at walls set to bear
on the imagined impinge
defense arising from
the experience of our
great Quixotic fear
of the unknown.
another kiss has passed
before, and me by.

Oh, Herodotus, Aphrodite
Fair. Kind. Sweet.
In Democritus too often
Found. Made. Seen.
A statue in an Honor's path

Remarks, Colossus, Alexander.
Aloud. in confidence.
Anthropological Reclamation
Deep Theory of Light, softened
whence Litotes Socrates?

How gentle a socialite's repast.
The mortal hours of material desire
Inside the construct of Heaven
The Sensual Hiding, Inside
a Blind caesura, like grapes.

Which wracked Greek
Wreaks wicked wrong
Whence wild wanton
meandering?
Wild melons float
In the duck soup lake
Thrown in the reeds.
Swan's Wing High
wondering
Geese well feathered lay
Beneath the surface
reflected light bends
and weaves the scales
murk and mud root deep
Sense the expanse
a Feast of space
as leaves seek to dwell
weaving winter's wan

29

Well collegiate days bygone
Happy, Rough and Honing
What a lack of wonder

Midnight Hours and Damns
The Self-right struggles
tearing of the world asunder

Down the harrowing then
stepping light to yonder
rolling social grace making thunder

College times to calm in
A walking working way
Too much, too little under

Round and Back again
Art Fair lit the process
of Language, History, Plunder

Direction walking lithe
to a goal now in sight
where talent's might to ponder

Finally the Ivory Towers grace
A real-time sense of place
And face not yet to squander
Yes collegiate times, alas
lost in vulgar, unjust morass
Planned in times as vast this blunder.

The raw sex of it
a waiting frill
Wandering underwear
Circulating blood

Wander wonderlust
this praxis forfane
Like ass stroking hand
And keeping things sane

a bitter corner to hold
darker inside to caulk
a passion abays
in plain social walk

walk past childhood's end
This ground-floor's Fair gain
on a foundation of lore
and of a motherhood gained

No small easy task
in this parlance to chance
as humanity's dance
holds our hearts in a still.

The Printshop
The Root Canal
Memories of my Uncle
Reside nearby with love
Uncle Tom, my Father's graces
And shadowed us in love
So odd the perchances
that have brought me to
these landmarks of memory
a power resides here with me
that belies the secrets held within still
matters not of my import
Though matters which the annals
will recall I influenced
Odd hope of family & hearth
in times gone by
a feeling of meaning
It is only the efforts
Which evade the questions
each of which
wonders why.

The redactive dream
a laughing Armageddon
once, only.
Yet now, the absurdity
repeals the notion freedom
not all these are free.
A clear demarcation
not reflecting ability preys
and reminds
The bifurcation abays
as it incites. Conflict
under auspice of protection
The inequality so plain
as to add Fuel to a fire
Wild mire
passing of days
Bangalore in Polka-Dots
a season of drugs
without easement.
Town Hall Meeting.

Love does not
require The deeping pain

The wracking nerve
The inconsiderate consideration
nor the prejudice
Love is Love
and not always easy
Simple
or plain

I will have mine plain
easy, simple
and not climb
That mountain of woe
Any longer

Reign Dear

Rocks moving moved
as tombs opened spin
and let me into this
odd morass of think

Think on it
as rock moves heavy
and in wetted air found
droplets of living
sometimes coming down

rock set of fires
fires keeping warm
and of destruction too
Prometheus bound to rock

Air and fire and water
bound of to the rock
a blue marble
in the eye of God.

NOT SACRIFICE IS GRIEF

letting go like a sacrifice
of some sought love near
That grasping, now hateful
thing
So unforgivingly clawed
from me. mine. as if
there was meaning left to me at all
as if
That now as stolen hope
Those verses true, that book
could represent anything
That, that had to do with me
to some abated death
who knows me not at all
and has none
      but selfish cares
and has none
      but hurtful ways
That letting go not the same
As grieving for my work
lost poems, lost wisdom

2% and then Olive
refracted light restrained
in a broken window pane
inside the grove of hate

Some mongrel gorgon

with dulled tooth and claw
eye wept to shame and blood

Casts her ugly shadow
empty of spawn and vile
nor kept as falsely fine before

the eaves topple down
as arches break and
as stones pockmark the floor

refracted light in
empty space

For Oppenheimer's Grove

What is this deeping sadness brings
of Futures hoped
or holiday bells
of this and that
or dire knells

Is it still the undressed
of bashful ways polite
where that helpful kind
has left of mind
The lack of mirth impressed

Death is it gone, so early
Doom it seems not your barly
Frame
Though a blazing planet sits
on this precipice

An echo of the joy of fate
near to fortune turning
of that I could relate

Leading into a vein of hope
like wealth to heaven
something inside points
to that grace of feeling
reminding, appointing
and conformed to space
shadows and light
and the remains of day
like the colors not blue
in dusking skies
feet on the ground
not seeking boots, warm
summer skies and lawn
to tickle – in the graces
each to form
with the extra work
not undertow
to save and saving
a breath, a leak, a life
and in Paradise round
to glow reflecting the sun.

Oh my Stars. Agained
in a place again before
Surprise – edly – ish
since befores as trodden
Most to recount, and odd
that must have been '87
yet, no – earlier?
That clock rings so real
Starting to think twice
yes, twice at least B4
not so very many more
I can let the with Wiley go
and yep maybe twice
and another, and above
so the shifting of space
a frontal renew
yet some of depths and
other
remains

Round – –
And down – –
Come around
to this town

Funkytown, now
run, running down
not final thrown
when the sound

bumps the sound
Slow up player
that road home
is no sweet clown

But laugh at the lawn
lookin' so unmown
dig in to the unknown
thrown, like for a

beat on my feet sweet
in the loving meet'n'greet
tweet my selfie twerker
not fab jerk gab
Deep like a mangrove
Swamping a floor
For some more, people
In a house with a steeple

Fish and loaves
So come in the droves
And hoof the cloves
Slide on snow

check the show
you know
that root so flow
the boogie going a blow

Laughing Listless Langour
Blink
Not a missing entried
Stuck
Charge light brigade
Sit
Horses running shoed
Bit
to the delight
with
In the dangling darling
Calm along the dawn

Some as a cry for help
Where the prize is sought
as in battles fought
and to win the peace
Warming-in somehow
And glow in gangling lines

little lights spark
and so of life bright
dotted like blue skies
taken a day at my time

The trees cut down and dragged
Into hearth can find
Some of a selfish warmth
and appointments atop

So when Jesus wasn't
left behind
that was no easy trip

Who wounded you so much
that you hurt me without concern
as if my life were a chew toy
set to exercise your toothy jaw
though, really, no matter that
question
The hurt you give fucks everyone
Beyond excuses
And, though once tried
no longer of any merit the effort
Learned of to discard a person
Such an unwelcomed gift
Such too to sift through
to find the signs of that poison
So my folly does not repeat
with another, if, or others
not a mother's gift
Just the vile bile
Of a toxic person
who is "Just that way."
I am better than that.

Rushing Rainbows Real
Shining sunlight seems
to pattern a waterfall's mist

Leap!
and in so falling up
landing leaned long
to fly

Rudolph, some horny
and slight sleighride
bellied up to plain plane
to decorate the hours

like the wave, waves
from warm and cool
on a seen scape

like meeting
on the pole, even north
Fun – da – ment

not now lost askewed
Such famous fail me
agains agains pain
and rail for the fail
and again and to hurt
Such of to understand
No more the hope in it
as if plain were not fit
to comport plain, commit
and no dearth of meaning it
Still the smell reeks
as some more freaks
not so Giant seek
to find a better way
by window shopping me
and then again to deride
a talent forged of pride
from meagre and aside
that block breaking
and more so slipping to

Folded flotsam set renew
and no longer just stolen
works
I had to say
of one imagined splendor
That you kept asundered
Secret to a love your own
not shared
not cared
inside, not live
So it goes when that gift
comes of its weight of it
like a child's fit or
tantrum
1 plus 1 is just that:
one plus one, and next 2
two only two like shoe
Only one, or two, or kinds
perhaps
For some no other Thoughts
and of Th'Antism
not all that wreath

Faith is an engine
The internal force beyond
The acrobatics of life
Somehow as close to birth
as to bridge life's passages
from 3-4-5 to all else too
and so too Love and of Joy
That lingering near veil
an apprehended grace
in a shape, of forethought
not the waste of as-fought
delicately to juggle not wrought
and so too shines in toys
a Leap Forward future's worth
of reflecting life and mind
and of such of souls
where a cognizance remains
embodied more than brain
in a Universe of living too
So of the blue of flames
Calming to think upon

Such young hopes at a doorway
Something true brand new
Such of kind importance called
That this is what we do
Colors bright and colors calm
the evensongs and the dawns
The sense of place carrying on
as we love and join in parade
the newness of potential's light
the gravity of a society might
in just such best ways' sight
a happily ever after

And to see those stalwart folk
New to a simple proving yoke
And barely settled in
confront the sensed of dire news
count the raindrops and read the dews
as the seasons shift anew
brought more depth into the muse
and a mother's edge of tears
and a father's conquered fears
So lightly touching future years
and so at a loss of now
and barrowed in before my eyes
the stalwart strengths of daily rise
whose secrets were never pried
slipped to the depths instead
where a simple sleight-of-hand
so barely seen did hold command

and spark a hope as in demand
to raise that force within
and in a quiet simple dance
in meager and in circumstance
embrace that from within
and ply those talents realized
in proper time 'neath money skies
to find that hoped path forward

A learning hard beguiling way
to ply a trade of yesterdays
as a luxury of sorts begun
with love-learned skills
so sharply honed
from door to door they kept our home
so gently moving onward
from rough spot to rough

and on Graduation Day
that proud Doctor of History
so as such to
that bridge to health
brief in the light, brief
and those shadows played
such reminding of whens
so briefly laid by the pens
with screens cleaned
and a classroom, or two
See the hill yet?
to seek that transit to

a middle-class enough
to feel belonging in this
United States
This our society where
families build on
struggles and success

So that lightning strike
came unbidden, faultless
where all such Doctors
whose teaching told of thens
were untenured, cast-out
as if by fickle fate
such of the plans that came
from decorous robes and tassel
back again to make words
and set the soul in motion
with pens and screens and
illumination
with a shattered dream
so there then dragging on
and the shifting from
social revolution
to an analysis of it all

Driving from an Arch
through Dinosaur Pancakes
to that place of my birth
to a room as understaired
and rough reckoning again
yet that time when to find
a place to live again as home
and the screens came out
in a basement
and pens to a writing desk
and this grandfathered boy
having had a small walk then
before
began again of weaving
life
So it goes of early years
and that such quiet plain
and those flotsam touched
when bacchanal, too dear to me
of roughnesses
and pens and screens
and, "NO!" and "Don't Touch"
and other errors of struggle

Such of Quotations schooled
and of Honors for others
Such of a looking-glass way
where of my own arts seen
through the mylar, a dream
of something more together

Apart ment, Apartment
Apartment Basement
Studio, Studios, Kitchen
There when difficult times
not always ease to ease

Yet, House
And House, studios
And a basement full of
the multiple makers
and of struggled for
to mat and frame them.

Boarding an Ultralight
Prayer flags streaming
wonderment comes
on the unknowing wings
of Garuda
As a flock seeks the
Train
Encamping Humanism
in a "Well done, well met"
This Tibetan Daze
Like a Singaporean Pidgeon Coop
Freedom's Light freedom

What is the
Need 'you' are
meeting?

Internal (Evidence)
External (Facing)

Mission Vision
         Values

CAN DO!
We can save
Hayes Valley
in an Earthquake
after (as

& Thank you
A personal

Champions of a Cause
Relationships

Substance a Theory Action
Remembered Flour and
a reasoned spirit forward
time and timing home
Home is where you are
who you are with and your
Community rests home
So Homes can Community
So communities can too
This is the effort
showing living
a Birth of Spirit
The blossoms of a spring
Showing colors bright
welcoming Future
a humor sometimes rare
like home, a sacredness
where the compass points
more ways than one

Wherein the lessons come
on a journey
from within and without
Seeming to a medium
that simplicity a trust
the open faith in our hope
The doorway there too
Some brilliant genuine trope
While offering true gentle clue
Must as mystic act
which sleight of hand abays
to a force weighted rust
lingering, wet, tedium
seen clear to remove the doubt
The suspicion of the get-to-know
waiting weighted embrace
to save the human race

So stress dull aches
Achilles limps my neck
and reptilian down
yet an achievement
red tape gates opened
and to the garden again

Oh strings hold true
where muscles remember'd
like wild quanta unknown
Chain matter mystic miled
raisin in sunshine shadowed
reason in lifetime

This future beckons 11th hour
yet again
yes it matters still
practicum primer prance
universal living dance
Spatial Survival

Bengal.
Polar Bear.
Session Man.
New Drawing Book.
Alligator C.
$24

Falling softly on Halloween's Shadow
a quest remains
quiet, wondering
Blending into reality so well
as nothingness seems

Falling softly on Halloween's Shadow
a doorway opens
a realm secret reveal
again in time reminds
as seeming seals

Ceiling
Falling softly on Halloween's Shadow
rising
as exceptions
Feeling
The Actions worked of hands

yes I reckon it is
Support divine of that
life amid

My ken of object motion
not wandering farther
feeling unreal

Physical
Process
death friendly finding
welcome joined

Snatching Sparrows

My Foot graces a bee's shadow
for a moment
I worry I may have killed
a pollinator
as water flows on asphalt
pooling in leaves

Sun shining Sunday Service
meekly again
wondering at quieted Force
with spokes waiting
to be trimmed to a wheel
of my making

This is an importance active
a missing piece
Joy of it in giving and receiving
a local solution
To the plainest difficulties
in my life

Wisping fog hung low
tiny starshine flowing,
as just to trick the eye
lightly frosted glass so fine
yet with movement's delight
the cool summer's early dusk
calls a hypnotic cool
along a cultured tree-lined way
Close to autumn as hawks fly
in a precipitous way
leaning toward dawn
as warmth starts a
      simple
      doppler
      fade to dusk
Orange skies wait
as crows fly speckling skies
looking for sunrise.

The author has lived in interesting times, caution, faith is a five-letter word. And Love.

To purchase *Poems* by Daniel Farnan
and a variety of other books,
please visit

www.apsssf.com

AMERICAN POETRY SYSTEMS
South San Francisco
California